UGLY DUCKLING PRESSE

Commodore
© 2017 Jacqueline Waters

Drawings © Selina Reber, from the series *Vokabular*, since 2009

ISBN 978-1-937027-91-9

First Edition, First Printing, 2017

Ugly Duckling Presse
The Old American Can Factory
232 Third Street #E-303
Brooklyn, NY 11215
www.uglyducklingpresse.org

Distributed in the USA by
Small Press Distribution

Distributed in Canada via
Coach House Books by Raincoast Books

Distributed in the UK by Inpress Books

Designed and typeset by
good utopian, Doormouse, and the author

Printed and bound at McNaughton & Gunn
Covers printed letterpress at Ugly Duckling Presse
Foil stamping by Hodgins Engraving
Cover paper provided by Materials for the Arts

This book is funded in part by grants
from the National Endowment for the Arts
and the New York State Council on the Arts

COMMODORE

Jacqueline Waters

drawings by Selina Reber

Charitable Trust 9

If I Get Taken Away or Like Snatched 10

A Child to the State 11

Heel of My Hand 12

Others Need to Get in Your Row 15

"I'm Entitled to My Opinion" 23

Candor 27

Stiff Hedge 34

Fear Not (Provided You Fear) 36

Don't Be Upset If You Don't Hear from Me 38

The Actor 39

The Tower 40

The Pentagon 45

Good Try, Bad Advent 52

American Songbook 54

Horsing Around with Your Boyfriend 55

Two-Time 61

Scissor Half 63

The Inalienable 64

Protocol 65

The End 66

It Isn't Easy … 68

The Holdings 69

All Ears 75

COMMODORE

for Evan

Charitable Trust

Give
Giving kills time
Pause giving
Like you're too important for it
Like if this
Is now a renegotiation
Then you'd prefer to suture up
Last year's money bags
And make everyone walk to the well

Or share
Sharing strengthens the teeth
Hunters are quick to say
Their relationship with their dogs
Is never mere ownership
Instead the hounds
Become part of the family
"We lowered him down with a golden chain
And every link we called his name"
Goes the song
About Old Blue
That famous old
Dead dog

If I Get Taken Away or Like Snatched

"I saw you called me yesterday
but I was talking to that roofer.
I tried calling you back
but I got your office
and, I don't know, your office
thinks you're a wrong number.
I'll be home tomorrow.
Thank you."

On the kitchen counter I find a potato with a Post-it note
addressed to what would have to be (she lives alone) herself:
"More potatoes in the garage." The "garage" underlined.
She offers to make me rice pudding, a ploy to use up a bowl
of cooked rice I've seen on the refrigerator's bottom shelf.

I don't answer, so no one does.

I put on "Strong Wind Through a Desert Willow."

"Extreme Rain" layered over "Diesel Generator."

A Child to the State

The way to do history
Is not to care about it
Whatever you care for you diminish
Facts remain the same, changing with the day
While what is true of one repeats
By turning true of another
Everywhere the sound of crying
Neither immediate nor interesting
Unlike you, with those low goals
You're not just going to overflow toward
You've got to list the ambitious pains
Persevere through the doubt you watch
Take inventive forms like clouds
Owing the world a form

Heel of My Hand

You are
as attentive
with me
as a friend
patiently
remove
first your left
then right
earphone
each time
my lips
part

Keeping
this attention
is key to
getting through
I think
or everyone
thinks (my
thoughts just
a bristle from
their brush)

You recommend
a delay in
investigation
(you say
justice

is always
best when
delayed)
as you press
the pen
to the
paper's most
unforgiving
places

You are
to me
a big "how"
(like no one
—they say—
asks a billionaire
why they made
2 billion dollars
they just ask
how)

Oh how I
used to think
I needed
someone to
hold my hands
to the piano
at the bar
that everyone
would rather
no one played

How I used
to want more
clarifications
and how I used
to want (I
cannot tell
you how
desperately
I wanted)
to call them
(the wants)
a surcharge

on the price
of admitting
to preference
for I preferred
you above
others
clownish
though it
made
me seem

Others Need to Get in Your Row

The place has water glasses and a pitcher of water. You pour for yourself, do your work, then you leave. If you don't, there won't be a place for someone else.

First day I wasn't there, something bad happened.

Then nothing happened for two weeks.

Again, something bad, followed by weeks. Of nothing.

I thought I saw a pattern.

Bought a notebook, started to write down incidents.

Most days I just wrote "no incident" and signed it "a friend."

Your first articulation will be of no use to anybody.

That is the law I labored under.

If anything I did can be considered labor.

Though I tried to make it all into labor, wanting rest, which I knew could come only after great exertion.

To get love, for example, you deploy contrivances.

Look good and talk good, without seeming contrived about it, while knowing love devalues itself in proportion to how well you police yourself to get it.

So love is stuck.

It uses dry shampoo.

Who uses dry shampoo? Love does.

Who had a tracheotomy? Love did.

Because I care about you, I say, "Well I heard someone died doing that, but I am sure you will be fine."

Because you care about me, you say, "All people have problems, though I have never heard of problems like yours. But you will work it out, I am certain."

It's normal to be nervous. Also normal to just stroll in unprepared. Strange this cohesion of warringly normal impulses, grouped up into a thick thought-absorbing crypto-layer …

The rain is pouring down all over my head onto my neck and basically out my pant leg
It's a cold rain and you know what isn't coming? The bus
Though it sounds like bus brakes hissing when a passerby asks
if I'm going in the direction of Lincoln
I'm not going anywhere I'm just standing
between two recycling bins getting rained on
Is it a crime, and if it were a crime, were it hot?

    Wild white bears

break the ice in pieces

and with their claws clear holes

through which they plunge

to kill fake fish

and carry them to shore

        So the development of humility begins

                with a strangely lavish

           waste of forces

Consider yourself in the aisle of an old church filled with old people.

You reach a hand down to touch your sack.

Your hand stiffens.

When you tap your stiff hand with your free hand, your stiff hand shatters.

Coils of dry paper.

For an ordinary person, everything is temporary.

Even the hand of god. Sometimes it includes a portion of the arm.

Sometimes robed, the sleeve gaping like the *Bocca della Verità*, that hole in the wall you wish in.

The law told me to stay involved, to run from reflection, to mirror others whenever I felt least at ease.

But I hated having to display a response. Especially when I could see it coming. Someone at the front of the line dropped all their money on the floor, or moved both hands around inside their bag feeling for a phone, and people caught waiting looked for someone with whom to exchange a knowing look.

I was not really knowing.

I was a burr in the paw of a bear creeping up on myself to slam the canteen.

I wanted to throw my coat at certain faces. March over and step on one's toes, grind my heel into a forefoot.

My plan was to keep showing up but start spying on everyone from the hallway. My plan was to enroll at a locksmith school in Arizona and it wasn't a good plan, and if I forgot to change it I'd automatically board the plane, like I was a program that would run unless turned off.

Others need to get into your row, they said. Do you pull your legs in and twist sideways

    or do you stand and hover

        hinging your knees

       over your seat edge—

You can't get around this in everyday life but you thought

       maybe you could

and you feel surrounded, as if by a class

one you are a part of

without having agreed

without adequate time to consider

the difference between

mere succession and real causation—fell down *from* the push

      fell down

           a moment after the push

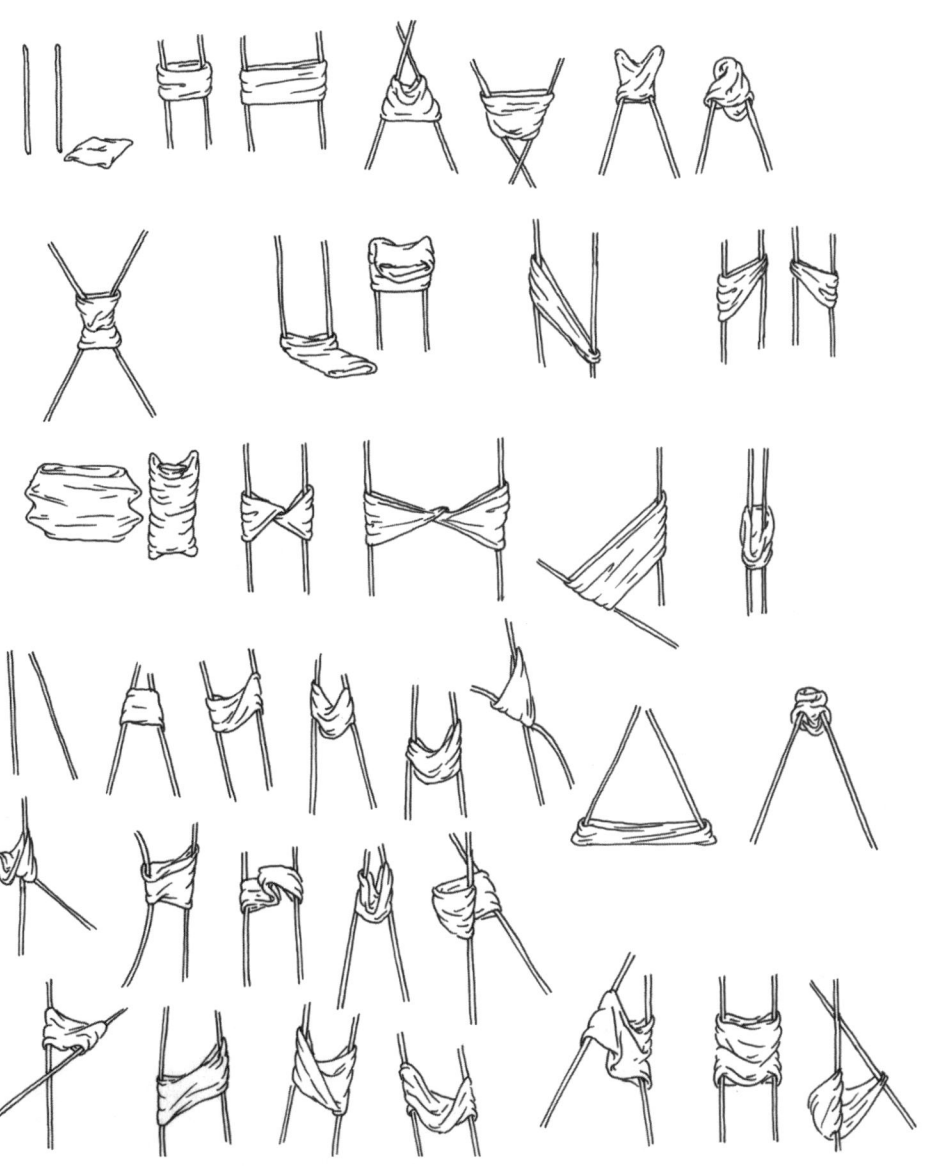

"I'm Entitled to My Opinion"

You also have difficulty with North, South, East and West. They don't mean anything to you. You can find places eventually through trial and error. You can figure out a map if you imagine yourself walking or driving on the map itself. You can see that the direction you want to go is "over here" or "over there" and turn that way on the street. Your dreams have known people, but their faces are not a factor. You get who they are, but not by looking at them. The truth is, you rarely face someone in a dream, and when you do, you just see a generic oval and some shadowing. Blond people are invisible to you, so you have to be extremely careful to not ignore them completely. It's as if there's nothing for your brain to hold on to. You consistently confuse the people you've placed in any given bucket: all women at work with shoulder-length hair are pretty much interchangeable, from the temp to the VP. You have often walked into large mirrors because you don't recognize your reflection and truly believe this other person will move out of "your" way.

Candor
for Filip Marinovich

3/2011
This seven-year-old yells well I'm gonna kill you at her friend
after a cold hosing
in warm weather. I can't stay
in this apartment anymore the domestic partner
has left and taken the mustard
and salt and other items you
only realize are missing when you go
to put them in food you wouldn't
have cooked if you
had known. You never
know. Things
get away from you as you snatch, lift, push and press
as at the gym where you're
the only woman and pretend
not to be looking when a man
fails to lift his weight, the barbell crashing
to the floor equipped to bounce it.
Vertigo: like the room you are in
is actually a ladle
the bowl of which
just tipped. I get it
whenever I turn my head to the left
while leaning over, or when my inner ear
is inflamed by something—a cold—the end of a cold—the manifestation
of a cold that doesn't otherwise occur—or just, you know, stress.
Consider Hopkins and stress, all the strain
of turning Jesuit and then those hard irregular beats. You shuck and I'll
gather, said I, when I was nine, given a ShopRite bag of corn

from a farm stand, for which a farmhand
stole hundreds of ShopRite bags it'd seem. Now the grocery carts
stop working if you wheel them over the invisible border
at parking lot's end. Invisible fencing
for food-collecting humans. It must feel good
to have someone worrying over you—I mean
wouldn't it? I like to imagine this person I went on a date with
worrying because I haven't written him back. It's one of
my best outlets at the moment. Don't get it
twisted, I say to him, imaginarily, in this outdated slang
that makes me feel I have a companion
in my head, one I feel
superior to. Don't get it twisted because I am not available
right now. I have a broken heart,
chief symptom of which
is a sense of neverendingness.
Why can't a human express pain
without saying it feels like I'll
never trust another person again, or it's like
I'll never feel such love again, I'll never
live with someone so good-looking. He was really
good-looking, don't you think?
Domestic partnering with someone
easy on the eyes,
someone whose looks
satisfy you, look to you
like the golden mean,
their proportions suiting you
and never irritating you—
the way your looks irritate someone
which you figure out when they
make unflattering references

to this part of you they also say
is cute. Like one of my people
thought I was short
and my skull
too indented at the temples
whereas this one, well with
this one the main thing I admired
was the regal shape of his head
which seemed like something to worship
if it's all right
to worship a shape.
All that beauty of others,
it changes doesn't it?
Consequently I'm going to get face lasers
when I get the money
these lasers they aim at your face
and make you beautiful
in six or eight sessions
spaced apart enough
to forget you look exactly the same.
In this river is a time of change
shape-shifting
ankle-touching.
Discomfort they say
well I say
is good for your art
because when you are hurt you will try
to repair yourself
with plastic means
architecting the poem
into a structure to hang
your heart on—well that's disgusting

how about a structure
to hang new feelings on,
feelings of danger
and reconsideration?
In reality this guy
I think he did Reiki on me
because he got to my grief
lifted it a little
up and sideways and I felt
like Atlas if he got to shift
the weight of the world a little
though why it feels good
to shift a burden I can't say
for before long it shifts
to a newly distressing position.
It's like waiting for the train
at night, you get tired of standing
and of leaning
so you try a crouch.
With my new exercise training I hope
to get better at the crouch.

4/2011
A box of unopened
herb storage pods
is there each morning to greet me. Why is it
extreme feelings
can only be conveyed
by insisting on their permanence (I return, you will note,
to this idea, with something like a hope
for permanent ideas): I will never
love again, I'll never

live with someone again, things that may
or may not be true. Some are true, like I'll
never again have access to this elaborate
water filtration system, nor taste of its
cool clean waters. I can get one
one day
maybe, if I really aim to, but it's more
the care another took
that feels like
care for me. You can live, you know
without being cared for
or cared about at all. It's not
a functional requirement, just
an interest, something that takes
the edge off, though you pay it back
in other, sharper edges.

5/2011
At eleven last night two cops
idling in a car at Venice Beach came
over the megaphone telling everyone
the area was closed and to
go home, repeating it like the voice
on the automatic train at the airport
warning you about your baggage
and people threw bottles at the car
and kicked the tires and the cop
kept talking saying the area is closed
and it's past curfew and the area is closed.
It's not true
about the area, I mean
I'm here

just I'm inside
a studio apartment
like it's not true the guy got anything twisted
though it's true impressions can change
the further they get
from conceptions.
Welcome to this, my "A Month by the Sea," a title
I say over and over, no it's not
a title it's a thing, a month by the sea,
that I have always wanted, and now look,
I have it. I should use
an exclamation point there: I have it!
And Filip I'm falling in love a little
OK a lot
with the guy from that date, would you
believe it? Now I'm not one
to do that kind of thing—
I am recently
heartbroken as you'll
recall but he sent me, among other touches, a link
to a YouTube of "Having a Coke with You."
So as you see it's not my fault, this falling
in love and forgetting to walk around
heartbroke. Filip! I am trying to write
in verse to you with candor but it's hard. As you know I
revise a lot to get rid of anything
resembling self-disclosure. Well, disclosure of the
ordinary self which implies
access to another self I clearly do not know.
Easier than candor is
affection which I hope will stir
the reader's self

if the reader is similarly
open to getting affected. Today I bought
an affected hat.
I wanted to look
like I belonged at the beach, I also
wanted to get protection from the sun.
So if I can claim I was being practical
then I can have this thing
that joins me to other
practical people
in no
particular fashion.
Some types of info
are easier to obtain
than others
about others you
need to know very little about.
Why do I strike out things
I think will reveal too much—
I mean in my other poems, not
this one where I am sort of
letting it all lie.
Well I say it's because
it's a distraction
from the interpersonal standoff I am
aiming for, which is true, but also
I'm afraid to "stand revealed," although
when I think about others I think
we are all revealed all the time, I mean
let's face it there's self-disclosure
and the author's attitude toward self-disclosure
that are always right there disclosed.

Stiff Hedge

If they ask you where we get our eggs
say California

It is your right to be lost
in your experience
as it is your duty
to determine
who's out to con you

Those eggs
are stupid
to your situation

As is
everyone
who doesn't respect
your past

You had to wake up
so early
pull paper bundles
out of a box
by a bus stop
pay
in coins
open the boxes
yourself
just to keep up
on crises

needful
more than
anything
of you

You (of all people)
get my mercy

I mean you get it
(my joke)

Fear Not (Provided You Fear)

A few people walk across the marsh
to whatever jobs await them
"Good morning" for lunch a burrito
wrapped in a microwave

break room pail full
of upc codes
their vertical blinds
not thrust to the sides
You can't forget
having to participate
in that phony hug

You think perhaps
she opened her arms
just to get out
of meeting your eyes
and you walked in

to that embrace
everything closing
around the lacquered sticks
crossed to hold up her hair
You said "a long goodbye"
to about half your self-respect
and leaned in
as far as she would have you

O unimportant Mars, why
do you think she did it?
Maybe she'd read something
about embracing your dislikes

or that which you pity
since you were all alone
at what had become a party
You stuck out
Your jokes taken seriously
though maybe you just seemed like a joker

and she thought, "I'll make a joke of her"
like if one of us strikes oil
the other drills at once
lest the first
drain the pool

Don't Be Upset If You Don't Hear from Me

Ranchers lease land from the government
At very low rates
That do not make up for the money spent by the government
To manage the land for the ranchers
Each rancher goes to sleep with a blanket
It doesn't stop there
Ranchers get sex in places we don't know about
The sex doesn't stop there
Ranchers were so mad about 200 coyotes loose in their area
So the government said OK we'll shoot them from helicopters
When the coyotes died it was OK
Because animals die all the time they are used to it
You like this cake I'll cut you a slice
A sliver
It's just a worthless sliver
If it were me I would be more circumspect about it
I would be less going on about it
I'd tear its branches off and act like I hadn't thought about it
Decorate the tree half and shove it out there to sit

The Actor

They broke it off
and gave it to me I
ground it to a powder
I mixed with water
in an old hated pail

Thus I gave them escape

Though after a while
they turned back: those people
know nothing of gratitude
and what you do
disappears

and may never
be heard of again
and you feel
(as an individual) annulled, given a role
of predictable passage
as though you were their weather

The Tower

Larry Rockefeller wants there NOT to be a tower built
in Englewood Cliffs, New Jersey
to hold and serve thirteen hundred employees
of LG Electronics, because from New York City
for example at the Cloisters
you'd see it looming over the Palisades
which the Rockefellers gave the public long ago as a green gift

but LG Electronics, in their defense, drew up what they say
are TRULY accurate renderings of the proposed building
which is to be sleek, glass and "significantly" wider
than it would be tall
and therefore (shrewd conclusion) cannot be called
"a tower" at all

Not even we
can hold the pole
on a line tense in the teeth of a sea monster ...

It's not like racing around
buying flowers for every short and tall pair of
women friends you spy—
there's NO idleness, not even enough of a lunch hour
to shut down the zone waivers
blow back all the dollars
wired here one way or another
based on a reading of shape—
though the New Jersey governor
(whose shape is all anyone talks about)

has taken no position on the project
floating sage above battles
waged by artists' skewing—
so like a cloud! So moveable!
Filled with the "hard-won" knowledge
position has convinced him
he's earned—born between vehicles
clustered at the tunnel's entrance
his name in papers
teeming with jobs
for construction-sector New Jerseyans, his days
asleep on the breasts of strangers—
those warm people cavorting, in minimal satisfaction
in the middle way of life

(And it was to be your home
when the angels dropped you to it—
  You were prayed over
  so very many times
  her palm on your forehead
  her other hand
waving in the angels
pointing out to them
ill parts)

It's probably our hearts. One day, from one drug or another
they'll beat faster
we'll go to throw it all in, every
greenish thing we've ever lingered over
seizing and grieving each tree
like that nick in the diamond's side that leaves it
useless for wooing anyone worthwhile

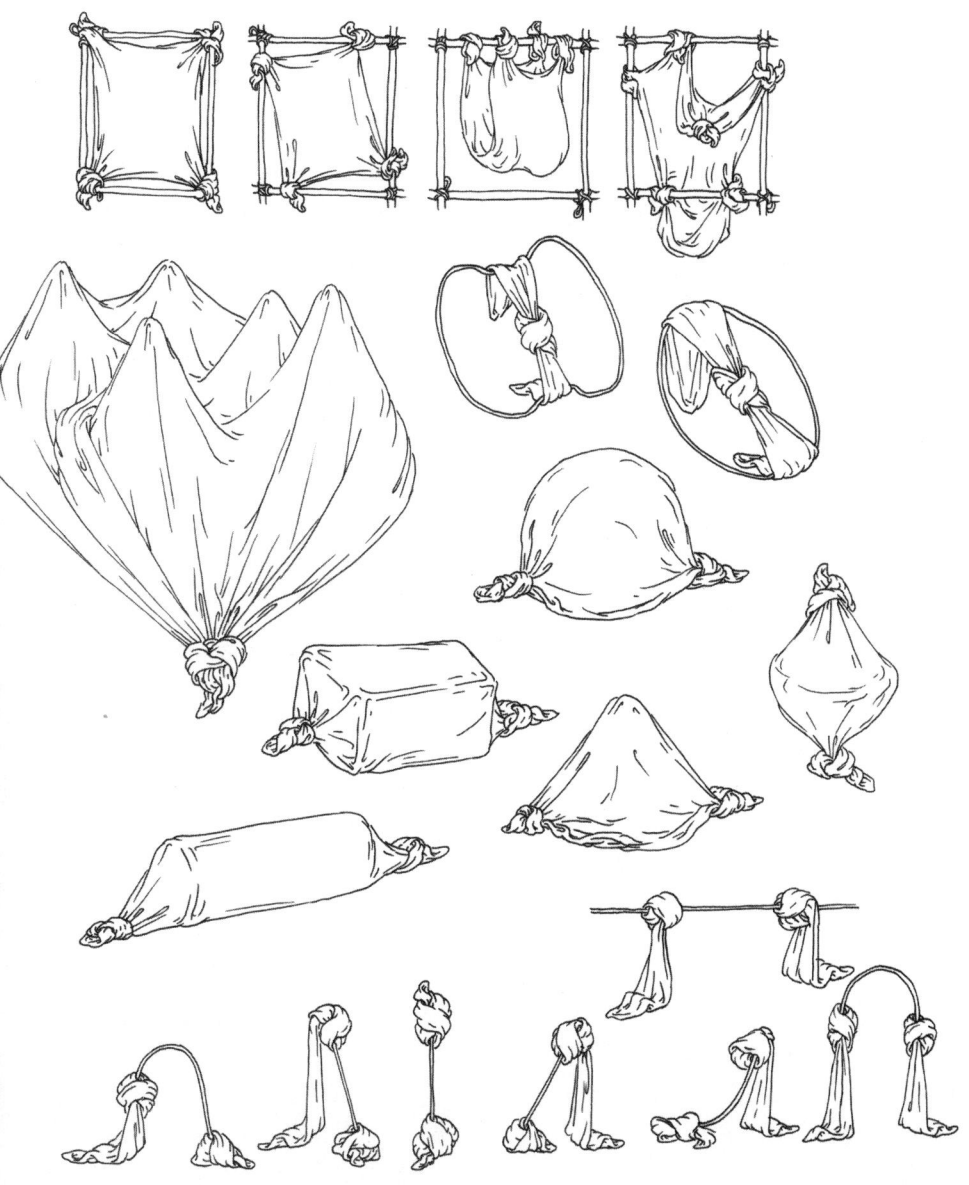

The Pentagon

A person has to live with the facts.
Say something critical—
tell everyone, for instance,
that you find your boss eerie
or a hypocrite, and it's you
who'll be associated
in your listener's mind
(more or less forever)
with eeriness, and with
hypocrisy.

No need to sign in today, he says. No work.
You find a stall and close the door. [Laughter]

—

I start by asking everyone what they think, he said.
I work it in there with their name
and a few things about hometowns.

This one, eyes closed, accounting for it all, drawing deep invisible lines past which one does not walk, retiring to a small apartment, reading a trade magazine before bed, a little tableau of vegetables cooling on an upturned lid …

The best way to open a movie, he said, is with an auction house scene.
Get your audience
to root
for a buyer!

—

You're alive. You tell the hotel clerk about a problem with the vending machine. She moves her face into second position, tells you to fill out a waiver and sign it.

If you're shy you're at the mercy of people
considerate of people who are shy.

One afternoon as you left the building you saw the supervisor chaining his bicycle to a parking meter. You stood there, outside the health-food restaurant. You said:

Hello.

And he said:

As if.

Again, if you're shy your main friends will be people interested in people who are shy.

—

This isn't
safe in
fact anyone
can easily
get at you

they'll search
your body

for two rows
each carrying
hundreds of

identical teeth
forced together
by a slider
hiding in its
throat a

Y-shaped
channel
and hold
something
hot to it

till you
break open
along
perforated
lines.

—

Or try sending sweetener packets
stuffed in little yellow
gratuity envelopes.

That's grace, the filled envelope.

That full meal
on that
sturdy plate.

—

We have to get this project launched before the announcement, they said. So you can see our problem here.

I can see your problem there. You're just going to eat a roll or whatever that brown block is.

An air of costliness: crumpled wrappers, torn cardboard, pried-apart plastic clams.

Treat all conversation as ad hominem argument, he said. Always think about what you might be able to find out about *them*.

Them. What Susan Noel called: *filler*.

Filler die. First the men of the family, usually, and then the women not long after.

Or it's the women who die, and the men live another ten or twenty years, being better able than women to do the business of living, and then the men die.

And then the children die, one by one, and their funerals are held on Saturdays and Sundays in buildings that look like houses but lie suspiciously close to the town center, on a corner, or main road, immaculate residences zoned as businesses.

Everyone takes a break, drives off in separate directions, two go
down to the quarry and walk, three to the mall to eat, several
carloads drive back to the southern section of the state.

A woman opens a crystal shop
in a strip of shops by the water.

She covers the counters with velvet, three chairs with slipcovers
of yellow and sea-foam green. The legs of the chairs she gilds. A
package of balsa wood paint stirrers

and pink edging brushes
in a plastic bag behind the shop as seen

from real-time satellite surveillance.
Behind the shop, ugh. Germs! The smell is bad.

—

You're looking through passenger lists, you're freaking out about
military records.

You open the inhaler and point it at your mouth for after you
figure out a fact. You thought you knew where you came from,
lulled by the family crest.

Keep copping to it, he said. You are a god and when you're
angry you stay angry whether or not bolts are discharged from
your fingertips.

You felt they owed you congratulations, if not interest on
it, since it had been months, and your achievement collected

attention wherever it was reported. Yet the department held back, and your supervisor, in particular, held back any recognition of the general feeling in the department that the department was holding something back.

You had said: there'll be a huge line. He had said: no, I don't think anyone cares.

—

She told him she would have to think about it. Meanwhile she was counting on him to keep her posted. He left her office with the sense of a decision having been made. He cleared some papers that had been left on his chair. It was supposed to be a paperless office, but occasionally it was there: paper.

If a teacher can lead a student to contradict herself, then the teacher's point is strengthened. Classic Socratic method.

It seems to be about asking questions, but its real purpose is to create confusion, to reveal internal contradiction and elicit self-doubt in the student.

But the student must interpret the feeling of losing an argument as self-doubt.

The presence of self-doubt as wherewithal to grow.

You grow as far as you may, then retreat. You retreat as far as you dare—

What a short day it has been! Still holding in our hands the

few poor flowers we helped each other to, the roast squirrel we
exchanged for a cold bag of apples

for who wouldn't want
a place to get well

a salutary place
to get sent?

Good Try, Bad Advent

I'm a file clerk at the insurer three days a week after school
The adjusters pull file folders
I return every paper to its place
Then meter all the mail and walk it six blocks to the post office
Before work I change into a skirt and turtleneck
in the junior high bathroom
Eventually the boss Beth takes me aside to discuss my appearance
Recognizable stains, she says, prove I've been wearing
the same skirt to work, every day, for months

In 1988 the ad asked, "How can you have more job satisfaction
in 1989?

L. Ron Hubbard promises a fresh look at today's problems …"

Do you know about James Arthur Ray?
He was this wealth guru
Attending his workshops cost everything you had
One day he loaded 24 clients into a sweat lodge
And brought in one fiery hot rock for each participant
You must want, relentlessly want
Hold your vision of new cars parked one behind the other
In your circular drive
Go to Phoenix and go without food or water for 36 hours
And finally sweat it out, converting wants
For food, rest, water
Into wants for wealth, consequence, import

But people started passing out
And were dragged by their ankles from the tent
Persist, he insisted, and overcome this waste

Until three died. Ray went to his hotel, took a shower
And called lawyers

He only got two years for negligence
But his real genius was after prison
He thought hard about what people wanted to hear from him
"What would happen," he wondered
If I took complete and total responsibility?"
Came the answer: "You would succeed"

Which if that's always your answer
It's fun to formulate the question
Like letting a hungry person
Laugh at all your jokes
Before taking back
Your promise of a meal
Proving you know
How to control
Another's body
In a completely
Sanitary way

American Songbook

It was Christmas last night in the
Bars very drunk. You had to tie their hands with turkey twine
Very high.

And seeing the fangs
Protruding from their mouths
Into four directions
Your own mouth showing
More and more fangs
You cried out
To your lord!
Some watchful, basic man.

Such a cry, such music, tipped
The scales toward you.
Bounty slid
From the scale pans to you.

So much goodness surrounded you
You sang through the songbook
Deaf to its warnings
Hearing only its beauty
Believing that beauty
Regulated you.

Horsing Around with Your Boyfriend

1.

You replied coldly
so as to disguise
a greater range of feeling

than you might like discoverable
in your mostly plausible
hoarseness

2.

Yet I'm more interested
in what befalls you—
not the things you do

I care only for the malady
and not its symptoms
sheared off like facets

from the crown
of a cut gem

3.

In love with the way you
never add your thoughts

   to the conversations
usually someone else
puts forward your ideas

   or something
close enough
this way you get

   to sit back and judge
the flaws in thoughts
you're no longer

   party to

4.

   They say by
combing our hair
and covering it

   with texturizing spray
gathering it
into a clean elastic we cross

   the threshold
into irresistibility
our looks

   need to be crushed
but no one
has the courage, the tallest around here so sweet

   the short we find them
quite kind
in-betweens

   as impeccable
with their dress as their manners
these are the adherents a god would want

   any god

5.

    Not to say women
are the birdwatchers of literature

    but entering the field
with an apology
for the lives

    you are about to observe
practically demands

reward, pulling
on the slip

to force the dress
to glide attractively

    across your legs
or to ensure
your clothing's

    apologetic
opacity

6.

Active searching, says Simone Weil, is prejudicial—

we must await the solution
that unearths itself

via wind and rain, or careless footsteps
or was it meaning

that unearths itself? "Seeking leads us astray," I
remember that much

coming forward to speak
in the tiny conference center, my voice

long since behind me
(like a passed knoll I could only

think of as "in the way")

Two-Time

The cities are emptying. Statistic to cite: rental vacancy rates.

Bikes are falling out of favor. Observe: black grit
                         across my forehead
               from the helmet's disintegrating foam—

    oh-so-ready
            for anything—last night I raised my fork
                inserted it into the dinner
    before the plate even reached the table—Why shouldn't I
have
    everything
             I want?
Why should not the sun
    shine harder on my bulk?

Toward you
    my heart
        beats
    at one-and-one-half beats per second
             having
    taken off early
to fill up on fluid, having
               parts hard and soft
       piling up parts

in the order they will be needed—
               I could have been
    a quiet little boy

>had I not glanced down the wrong road
>hollering like something's
>holding me back from there

At the time I put:
>"I sensed a victory so complete
>that wild wolves on me would eat
>
>and angels
>move to mount them"

Scissor Half

You were telling me your dream
at some point you started
just making it up

Thus believer and unbeliever are brought to heel

I hate it

But allow it like a veil between my heart and mind it would be
boring to lift

Really I've got to find a place
to lie down and go to work

I'm OK, I stand up and take my time
which I also accrue

Regret fixing the problem
but persist

I feel good about my persistence
(which I also ridicule)

The Inalienable

See that? Note
her behavior

but do not speculate
on her motivations

Hoard your observations

Be attentive in particular
to sensation

but do not interpret
the existence of feeling

as incentive to act

You're now just
a simple figure

better described
as a piece of furniture

You love carefully

You are careful to behave
as if loved

Protocol

I enjoy reading this book about giant waves
Penetrating so many secrets we've no breath left for the unknowable
The cold can balanced
on the half-ajar door
                          or how sometimes when we're laughing
                          I can't tell what we're laughing at
People, too
        are going to *party* tonight, you said, lining the staircase
        with potted forsythia
your 18 pounds of towels
absorbing
64 ounces
of eco-detergent
from a crack
in the bottle's side
                plus a carton of a hundred
                canned sardines, a couple of downed limbs—
                      that analytic lever newscasters use
                      to gauge an evening storm

The End

He told the story heartily
like everyone   who ever
       heard it   had laughed

No man from his generation   he (our
teacher)   added
       would ever walk into a room
and consider any woman there his
       "intellectual equal"

He just wanted   to entertain us
but we took   that entertainment
       more seriously   than we took
his having wanted it
       a fault of our   negative reasoning

At the time I had a job   opening entries
for a De Beers diamond
       design   contest

I was to reject any design not
       sketched with charcoal
       any paper mounted   on an incorrect thickness
of foam core board   Really my job

        was to get   as many
entries into the trash
as I could

They say the bomb   of your central question
    will tick inside the head
of your reader
       and someday that tick   will widen
          commandeering
what amounts   to miles
    of rich, tillable soil
        or grim, bloated swampland

None of us will ever
    feel   comfortable saying
    that this is it: the end

An end (let's summarize) is
    a consequent
with nothing else after it   or not a LOT—
    as the sign in the harbor says
       "NO WAKE"—
your boat should sort of   trail away
without affecting bathers   or other
    small craft

It Isn't Easy ...

It isn't easy to eat
at a table where no one
is eating or seems ever
to have needed to eat.

Eating is the same
reincorporating process
as reading, but reading
activates the tongue
only for the first
two or three years.

You're lucky
you're my book.
You are sick
of motioning
so you probably won't
wave me over anymore.

Left hand hails
a trolley. Right hand
covers the mouth
that could eat a trolley.

The Holdings

It was only when I really believed
I might lose it that I began
  to look at it, visit its farther corners
take longer in
angrily assessing them

A believer wants advice, instruction
not aids
  to reflection
not a shut lake flowing back
from the pornographic border

for most often our eyes
are open, we see
  our surroundings
as they are, we watch
as our "roving" eye

papers images
meticulously milled
  from our weaknesses
over the world, filling it
with the population

of our dreams
the way a polished doorknob
  fills up with a view of the room
—until you tell yourself
as others have told you: "Stop dreaming."

And this admonishment
is often directed
　at disobedient students
who will eventually drown
in rhetorical questions

like "who do you think you are"
which can lead
　to "what gives you the right"
and although when you
were nine years old

no one asked you
what gave you the right
　by the time you were thirteen
you were occasionally asked
who you thought you were

which continued
until you were about eighteen
　after which you no longer
seemed to think—
your sinful attitude

good only for monitoring
everyone else's
　scrupulously warded-off mirth.
Go, pluck the fruits—the trees
will not fall down, your heart won't

fall down to meet them—reach for
more to see and feel

   beyond that to which
you have grown accustomed—
more to say and yet the saying

   forces itself toward us
like some cheerful, unasked-for
  dawning, its arguments
separated only
by a hard push

   on that one word's
outward-facing ridges
  as though you can't just feel
with the whole body at once
but must extend an arm

   or its hand
to confirm the item
  has a shape
that the motor sounds exuberant
rather than intrusive

   in fact exuberance
is no longer inside yourself
  but outside
feeding on whatever you have
left behind for it.

All Ears

First thing you go for is emotion, because people can connect
with emotion.

It's not true
but no one's heart is in it, it just lays there on the table, overcome,
refusing to do the job of its own redemption.

—

        A seated audience

    gives up the use of its legs while it listens.

Many also
    lose awareness
    of their mouths closed against the exhalation
        that will accompany your instrument's
    return to its resting place.

Your own pills, someone else's water.

You saw me coming, but you didn't lift a finger.

Little brains like nuts.

Who ate in some dump off the parkway.

Who chose, from among the fruit,
two bruised specimens.

—

Not everyone
is controlled by shame. More should be, but often we feel

too ashamed for them
to effectively shame them.

It's not true, but it's what science says, or should say, nor will any science serve, the one we're ordering uses as analogy venereal disease and drags forth into the light any sense of animal kinship that has not by age thirty-five abated.

—

When you talk
you don't want to lie
but you don't
want to tell the truth
as you've actually calculated it.

The best way to hide something valuable is to hide its value.

I will keep saying, *This is the way we have seen it*, and I will brook no response or argument. I will absolutely not change my mind, because it is my mind, and my allegiance must be to it, or my words will have no use to you.

To whom do the scientists give bananas? The very useful monkeys.

People of the future, I resemble you
I am more sure of this than you

and yet you outlive me
(You've outsmarted me)

—

Centered in the display of pens
is a small paper pad
stuck to the rack for testing.

Generally squiggles, occasionally
the well-formed word.

I had spent the week working like a dog (which is not to put down dogs).

Later just hanging around the house maybe soaking in some bullshit postpartum herb bath.

Checking the stats on homeopathic galactagogues.

Friendships form as each person finds the courage to memorize the alliance. Its risks, its contours, the flaky ways you earn and lose faith in each other adding up, over time, into a grace: familiarity.

Suppose you use a line like, "I love you, but I don't really know you."

Or, "Town is that way."

Like moving the head
a millimeter to see what the bars have been obscuring all along.
Two millimeters
and the next bar will obscure it. One millimeter.

—

I've never liked going anywhere. I get nervous the moment before leaving. Though I enjoy the planning.

I don't enjoy the planning, but I am drawn to it, which is a type of enjoyment.

It was a rare farm. She flinched whenever something neared her ankle. Pecked too close. Animals, animated by demands. An animal came up and demanded her files. But they are my files, she said.

You won't get anywhere by protecting your materials.

You can judge people by the anecdotes that occur to them. You may as well start asking, what's your most memorable story about a laundromat? What humorous comment do you have about foreign menus? You may as well start

forcing them out—these automatic emissions—
provoke the associations, initiate
the arc.

I felt like, maybe he was a phony. Maybe the feeling of being his friend was the thrill of subjection to flattery. Oh *you*, he'd say, you *would* say that, and I'd laugh: complimented.

Don't wait
on the threshold, don't
come in the corridor.

Don't
have the fantasy,
the room
at capacity.

Individuals will stop to see someone
produce almost anything.

While crowds will press on and on
through a pair of saloon doors
they only partly control.

You're a great commander, believe in yourself.
You have my heart: you've earned it.

When you get to the top of the dogpile, stay there.
Even if all that entitled you to the top
is a late arrival.

Pledge allegiance to late arrivals.

Do you find me knowledgeable, do I have the persuasive recall
of a well-rested bookstore employee?

Now that I am a mother I grocery shop from other people's
carts if I need to.
Not if I need to.

I do it if I
find myself doing it.

—

So they're blockading highways
threatening to blow up milk plants
derail milk trains even
beat milkpeople unconscious
crash bottles of milk together
just to assure
a fair and stable
price for milk.

I am alone in this room where someone has left me a fan turned high aimed at my form feigning sleep by a thermos of water. I am almost never alone. I am never alone without

consequence.

We have to get this project launched before the announcement. So you can see our problem here. Plans weren't delivered till last night. And none of the documents will open.

I can see your problem there. Clients get angry. Businesses go under. It's a crime. It's really just criminal that they can do that. And then you have no choice: you have to shop there because it's where you shop.

I was investigating the—You're just going to eat a roll! You can save calories like that. By thinking of it as an empty sandwich. Slicing it but just putting it back together and

eating it out of your own hand.

Now I feel something.

Something biting me.

It's just the wind—It pricks, he says. That's the way the wind is here.

That's what's up with the wind.

To make a story a story, some event from the past must intrude into the present.

A story about the taking of a trip.
The discarding of something
found in the luggage after the trip.

A story about a funeral? I pictured a bigger house
and better food
when the caller told me
he'd died. Instead this cheap

late-afternoon spread, plastic forks upended
in a paper cup, cut celery sticks

dried out at both ends
and not even meant as a metaphor.

People of the future, I resemble you.

Like you, I wear in my heart what I read.
Like you, I didn't eat it because
I was hungry, I ate it
because other people were hungry.

You want to feel like a voice is talking to you
but not
as at a séance
secretly
cooperating with you.

This is just
a circulation notice, please do not reply
or call branch, or anyone, no one wants
to pick up a phone, it's like
touching your ear to the worst slice
on a chore wheel.

In cynicism, we believe that kindness
comes from weakness, understanding

from fear of differing, and compassion
from self-obsession

                          and this made your caring
feel solicitous, and my movement away from you
a tunneling under to truth.

                    If I can ascribe you
these motivations, I can
devalue your love
which frees me to seek
                more, elsewhere,
and to capitalize on the attributes
you discovered in me, named, called *good*,

and convinced me I had—that another, or all others,

would love my body
                    as you did, and that hands on me

would feel the same, and I could choose another,

a *better*, someone I put
above me in this world, whose success I could ride along on

whose illustriousness
would seep onto me
by proximity

that I may at last communicate *emphasis*
without dependence on *vehemence*.

—

A lament, she called it, and said to notice what you envy,
because it's what you need to grieve for, and it's what you'll
receive once you do.

I envy my neighbor in his garden wailing

frightened

that the fasteners could not hold
nor could the top, bottom or sides
and form is leaking.

Disaggregating.

If those aren't bites, then my only souvenir here is the shame
of my irritation.

And though I've incorporated it, I haven't quite brought it to
bear

on the decisions I need to make

regarding the future
and my suitcase

a roll-aboard I pull along
though the wheels
choke on the carpet's pile.

I am grateful to the following publications, in which some of these poems first appeared: *Banqueted, Chicago Review, Clock, Dreamboat, Elderly, Everyday Genius, Fanzine, Harper's Magazine, LIT, Little Star, PEN Poetry Series, Prelude, The American Reader, The Rumpus, VLAK, Wendy's Subway W/S, With+Stand.* "Stiff Hedge" appeared in a chapbook produced for a Private Line reading in 2012.